WILD CRAFT

Living Poets Press Inc.

New York

Published by
Living Poets Press
838 Carroll Street
Brooklyn, New York 11215

Some of these poems were published in Kayak, Choice,
Undine, American Poetry Review, Sumac, Epoch,
The Nation, Southern Poetry Review, Streets, Goliards,
Tennessee Poetry Journal, Damascus Road, Measure,
Jewish Dialog.

ISBN: 0-915726-02-5

For Laurel and Doris

Also by Allen Planz

Poor White and Other Poems

Goosetree Press (1967)

A Night For Rioting

Swallow Press (1969)
Chicago, Ill. 60605

CONTENTS

Offshore

I go to sea, before dawn, wondering
what else wanders these waters in the dark.

I had dreamed of people
walking down through the headland forest,
the groundfog shimmering over the paths
and lifting as the sky lightened.
At the shore they gathered
to hear the dawn begin
singing in the inward rushing of the sea.
Now I know the meaning of dreaming
is changing in our time,
like the names of God.

How I like to be at sea at dawn!
Headlands behind me rearing into light,
sift and saw of the swell,
girl-laugh and gull-cry...

alone in this stillness
knowing we change
and affirming
for out to sea we change
and change ourselves
forever.

During the Autumn Migrations

1

So many creatures I know shit in great fear.
The woodrat I caught in my gloved hand,
a muscled bolus squealing, the squid
evacuating its graphite ghost when I reach for it,
the blowfish balooning, needlejets at both ends,
the goosefish, head bigger than body,
seizing a swan in a backwater
and both making a terrible racket as they die.

2

The horizon divides & rises: a line snakedancing
quicksilver, beading forward: rafts of ducks
& geese in the thousands winging down the continent.

Now in the dark coves of dawn the shrill orange
crump of the magnums.

3

All day a girl sitting in a willow tree
drifts in & out of the islands of rain.

4

Oilskins dolled up with gurries
we charge into tiderips erupting with bass & blues.
10

Squid under fire. Trapped. Even trying to fly.

Under us the seavengers, groundsharks & lobsters
eating a hail of shredded tissue.

5

I take gentle inland poets out,
David, Tom, Harvey, Armand,
wild men! in ecstasy or fear
bellowing for blood or beauty
I can't tell which.

Bob catches a sea robin: a fish
with the armor of a chinese demon
& the fretted wings of men who continually dream of flying.

6

Birds, friends, fish gone,
the racoon on the roof of my house
grips its face with both paws,
& judges me.

7

A squid with her long arms
bears me a seed.

8

Silence: a diet of ice

Fasting: famine

The North Atlantic Drift

The dolphin in the sea
beneath my dreams swings ahead of her shoal.
I feel in the wieght of the continent
glaciers calving icebergs
and magnetic north unship from its fastness.
A groundfog of bone-chips and chlorine
hides spring tides seizing talus from cliffs,
and once I hear a quavering as of breath
as she passes, undertowing eddies, near
the boat I've made of glass now crazed
with the mesh of its own breaking.

Whinings, chortles, thin reedy cries...
a stiller sea. Waves hesitating far offshore.
I have known two passages underwater,
path of bloodbeat, path of polyp;
now I have survived the sea all night
rocked by the bodywaves of a creature
who has suffered me to make it real,
as I wake to the gill-bright headlands
where the arms of the dreamer
fold forward as he falls from the wave.

Mayday

1

There's been a shadow growing in my blood
since last I killed. Off Shagwong Reef
the sudden, incredible
swell turned wave, climbing humpbacked
among the fishing boats, one skiff
wild on the crest, breaking.
I saw the man in thunder
thrown spreadeagled. Off Ditch Plains,
off Cereberus Rock, off Ram Head
he picks himself up in surf,
seaweed on his shoulder, his nose bleeding.
I hear a shout and kick a clutch of vapor
to probe a slick
too deep for sounding, too cold for diving.
Darkness my love
lie naked on the shoal risen overnight,
that each dawn dies in my hand, its teeth in my flesh.

2

Yellow the color of froth bubbled from the crab's mouth-parts
yellow the first flag of rust on the dunes
the dead blue-green algae swelling the backwater
the stain of bile seeping thru flesh
the shudder of jellyfish, between pulse and disintegration
Ai! tellow the prong of the reef plummeting downward
the fog abruptly swirling out, covering the behavior of wrecks
the fog pouring out of the headland cliffslide,
                              granite boulders gleaming
the man coming towards us, waking with each step.

I am following
the strange roads the fog makes
thru the forest before dawn,
past a grinning possum,
an orange newt wrinkled under a fern,
a bat hanging upside down and glistening with moisture.

As I walk
I strip the years off a branch,
back to the heartwood, pit and scar of birth,
nearly a moon in my hand.

Twisting and turning
the fog moves on.
Go this way, it is whispering. And that way.
And this way!

My buried life rises from a seabed
and swims thru many seas, each one
saltier, looking for its shadow
or a tree of salt.

In the farthest reaches of the fog
a girl is walking.
When she turns, waiting, I see
the wound in her side.
Her hair and eyes are the color of an albino spring.

This way, she says, taking my hand,
and the darkness begins falling as the light had failed,
in air and in water, failing
everywhere the same.

Behind the quiet dusk
I am standing in

there's the mass thrown down
by the shadow of a man.

Earth shifts
its grip on it. The sea
skips a beat.

Faint track on the sand dune,
scar on a girl's breast...

While I stare in sleep
it goes faltering from the wave,
its center a splintering of fishes,

and over the reef the groundswell sweeps,
unbuilding just before breaking.

Moon Northeast

The moon is riding the cold northeast wind,
driving it wilder
with a bunch of vanished stars for fuel.

I remember all the journeys I've taken
but not their destinations,

moving on the road, the mountain, the sea
uncaring
as long as it is into fields
with that moon in my arms,
into cities rising open to its light
to love & leave behind.

This is the moon
that breaks & passes the stormclouds
which by dawn would be raging here,

and that first gave me the joy
of not wanting to live
forever.

Osprey

1

Once, lying all night
in the warm body of fog,
together
in the dawn
we felt a fault of silver open on the shoal,
we dove and reared
in flurries the ride ringed and raced away
as our dream of dolphins
left us shining
by a star suffering its birth offshore.

Hearing a cry,
a shiver deflected underwater,
we looked up
to see two ospreys freewheeling down the dawn,
in the enduring fulness of ecstasy
we glimpsed only
in the beauty of each other coursing currents
upswelling to that light.

2

I think of the men I work with,
artists able to get along
only by hustling their skills to the rich.
Having found the land again they try dreaming
it whole and always at the splendid
parties they stare past you at the sea.

They grow old gently, their women are transient,
their half-remembered children
live in distant cities.
Once in a while, high in a seaside villa,
the rich view their bone-breaking, impoverished art
and say, dig it!

3

"The otter dives but the osprey never misses".
I wrote that---and lied: they miss
terrifically, wing over tail hurtling,
to rise sopped in foam, limping
for power on strange astonished cries.

Now, drunk of DDT, they disappear
from the coves and estuaries
where they climbed the dawn first
and hovered, trembling, for the stoop
or hunched and hissed
if I came near their eggs
from whose thin shell the beaked and hooded creature
would not stir ever.

4

There's not enough light
but, still drunk, I get up anyhow
and go to sea. Black skimmers
start homing in, gulls flap
and gawk, the tide turns against itself
sighing. Then I hear a familiar cry
and know I am not awake.
18

And still
straining for dawn I hear, high overhead,
wings echoing
unfathomably down rift and reef
a shadow moving on the continent,
and I feel
hearts more perfect than my own
resound the sheer coastwise tremor of a star,
and I wake and die and breathe again
within the song a girl sings to herself
thigh-deep in a summer sea.

5

When a man dies, a bird is born
underwater,
only a wing at first
circling a tiderip, then faster
until it breaks free of the sea,
a fierce bird pursuing a cry into the northeast wind.

But when a bird dies...lies! lies!
The Suffolk County Mosquito Control Commission
spraying poison
wants only
to control mosquitos,
and the rich only their homes and their lives
ordered like great art,

and Mike Wright, painter, only to sketch
the birds that flee him in the saltmarsh,

and I only want to fly
underwater,
fainting backward thru a wound,

and a girl only
to be awakened at dawn, to swim out
thru fog brightening each instant,
and see the ospreys in their dalliance
soar in the sun
overflowing the North Atlantic,
hawk's eye and hawk's heart.

Bluefishing

In 1960 a steel spoon took a six-pounder off Monmouth Beach
that bent my rod at the butt for good.
Two three-pounders hit a popper off Bostwick
& cartwheeled in tandem fifty yards.
Parrtheads jigged thru Shagwong reef in 1968
took blues to ten pounds till tackle gave out.
A seventeen-pounder slashed thru
a school of herring to grab the Hopkins spoon
I was trying to snag them with.
A four-pounder in 1964 bit my finger to the bone
when I reached for it.
Another with treble hooks in its jaws
slammed into my knee
& sawed its way to my ankle.
A seven-pounder disgorged its last meal in fury
& bit a wood darter in half.
I lost four lures in ten minutes to a school
in Plum Gut. An eight-pounder
rose from 80 feet of water trailing 300 feet of wire line
& shook off. One wild night at the rip
a twenty-pounder had me raving of giant bass
until I slung it aboard
stiff with disbelief. Last night
off Cartwright the biggest I've ever seen alive
jumped six times
& on the seventh spit the lure at me
& leaped again & again.
Free.

Swimming in a Tidal Creek

Light enters the water with me   .

Shadows disintegrate
                         in a flight of killifish
and mine starts from the bottom
only a smudge   trembling   .
Silt streams from seatangle rippling downstream:

Letting my last breath sink me deeper
I float   the way of a turtle
     feet trailing   heart pounding distant surf
till a bluecrab snaps open its claws
ready to play hockey   and backslides to its eyestalks
     under the sand   .

                         Frogkicking off
I tunnel up to do a barrel-roll
and surprise
               a black-crowed night heron
studying the toil of fiddler crabs giddy
from holding the world with one claw   .

          Called deeply
                         go deeper

(I call you from your clothes   .

And
you come shedding gravity and shadow
goosefleshed, into my arms and we capsize tents of foam
You come   .
                            We dance the heat of one cell,
shell within shell   .   suntide   .

Bodywaves uncoil from a brainstorm   :   two lisps
of light we drift the bottom of the sky   :   sun
in the thinness of sleep slips from wave
       to mouth   breath to blood

Noon: needlefish misfire in static
from shrimp pricking a pool,
the kingfisher skids his ratchet along the bank
where a pine stayed in deadfall
rows one bought through a glassy glide,
an eel riffles the staircase of a leafy ear
and snakedances wind and wave opposing
---now you teach me the way of a creature
waveplaning a pulse variously alive

and hold me as the sea, in flames.
The current touches us with many tongues.
I know the speech of water, I could
utter it if I breathed it, if I turned
and lived in the word water undertows
and stresses between two halves of this world.
Now its stillness breaks deep in my brain.
I am more than one animal but only one being
as again I find wandering in your blood
the star I wake to in the hour before dawn:

So as the creek whiles away into the bay

    hand in hand   we somersault,

alight on a sandbar,
                    launch forward again,
refracted,
            and tumbled end over end,

our slick brightening about us,
                            darkness rising
around our shadows,
                upwardly shimmering

and for the first time we speak
and begin swimming, as dolphins rolling shoreward

bring home the dearly beloved dead, in praise of summer

Mako

Cleaning Mako shark stoned in firelight
I catch fire from a brainstem
where blood is darkest in my hand,
dark as the underwaters it hurtled from
blind to the flying gaff.
I have killed & I have slaughtered
in no name but my own & still I raise
the great head to the sky, prize open
the jaws to show rows of teeth
staggered like a tank trap, & feint
left in a circle at a school of stars.

In a ring of trees underlit by fire,
my knees in guts cascading from the carcass
uplifted in my arms, I lurch keening
for the moon that drags me out to sea,
moon I never dreamed but
as a bloodred disc occulting in my heart...
now this bloodlord of the sea I feed on fire.

Waking

1

I come to know
the night's violence slowly,
feeling this ancient, tubercular tenement
profile the street traffic,
hearing the old man a wall away
cough, shifting the iron of his gut,
seeing how soft they lie
curved in upon each other,
wife and daughter,
who might go on sleeping thus
forever.

Dawn's tiderips on all surfaces:
whatever can't
stay still or asleep
will be carried off, laughing, over the edge of the world.

2

Waiting for steamheat
turned off all night,
at a window
I breathe smoke downdrafted from chimneys,

and I imagine my lungs' tarred walls
readying, at another breath, to break into flame,

I remember the kiss of teargass,
the bell of darkness
beginning to beat
while I was yet twenty feet underwater.

Now I am watching light
flaying a creature whose flesh
peels off in scrolled gangrenous strips
till nothing remains
but a malarial stain
that a dancer, one of many coming forward,
leaps over,
into the sun the city skyline
refines down cross, spire, and frosted tarpaper.

And someone is dreaming me dead
and resurrected, a nucleus
of light shimmering
on a girl bathing in a sunfield,
a swath of rooftop wildflowers
suddenly stilled, a wingfeather
drifting above a smokestack
blackened in a hail of cinders

and disappearing in a laugh,
a god's or a girl's.

3

Last night my daughter rose from her bed
but not from her sleep.
She lived her dream in my arms,
eyes open to the danger that was killing
her father,
while I cried awake! awake!
till it was over,
whatever is over
when neither hearing nor seeing lies
in a body born of a body,
flesh of my flesh, fire.

Thru grease that soot has hatched on the window
a sprig of light advances
and plays on my closed eyes
one fit of burning:

the sun of the city
is passing thru most earthly things,
thru the dreams of the dying,
those staring at the skin
of silence
drawn from the glassy fats and membraneous metals
a morning lets in.

Darkness wets darkness
underground, a speech
touch finds on stone. All holes
suck sunlight and sing,
before birth, for water
dividing itself into waves
as heartbeat by heartbeat
I, hunting my own death
become an eye of the city, in blinding light
watching the forms of itself
about to break into flame or breath,

each surprised in its cell
by light coarsening the borders, voices
lost in the instant of waking.
Then, in granite, a pulse flutters and stops.

And darkness closes with darkness
and announces what's being taken, who's being had.

5

Once in the Tombs
a homeless man slotted for rest
on Welfare Island
raved and cackled of my fasting
while eating our meals.
"First comes the bread, said Brecht,
then comes the moral, that's what
I learned the years listening
in Union Square."

And we sat laughing
at the joke of this world
till they took him away
thru the cells stacked in columns
and vast files, where men rode
the fate the State had willed them,
having no other edge
against time,
and I turned to my hunger
wondering if I held burning within it
a gun or a girl.

6

A wall away an old man cries out
for dawn, every morning
since the world began with a wild song,
stars perishing, seas unbolting bells.
The sky roofed out of a tenement
sleeps in the flesh
of an old man
to wake in mine when I hear
him groan
and shuffle in his bed, who dies in his sleep

when the walls jolt
to the diesel clarion, but don't come down.

So I move to the motion of walls and men
almost dancing, almost knowing
what else has burned in my sleep
if so danced at a death.

7

An image flaking off storefronts
the catburglar alights among pigeons
who rise to a nerve in the sky
wavering like a vein too deep for needling.
He lies down with those who now suffer
rats and roaches to come onto them
scrimmaging, as the plumbing retches
and the elevator grumbles to the top of its shaft,
about to break down or break bread,
summoned by nobody.

Light enters time and alters
a nimble angel beginning its firefall,
dawn hemmorhaging thru the smog of sirens and carcinogens.
I breathe to give my heart away to the west,
a woman.
West is a woman I wound in my sleep.

Sharks

1

At night they come true
From offshore
they come when darkness
rises with the tide,
my time, strength, thought,
all but my life theirs
for the taking.

A jolt: the strike.
The dream of the surface
shatters and knits
to the shape of a creature
moonfishing, spraying wisps
of phosphor, its wake
a seamed hump of fire,

and I yield, as it dives
downtide, to a power
that can launch any being
netted by air and blood
for the wind to house
since heaven will never,

if not in measured test
let slowly erode until
the moment of straining
against each other: dead
still: creature against
creature, each curved

back into its darkness,
darkness against darkness,
viviparous, terminal.
The moon commands things
of fear to dance, first
apart, then together.

    11

Once, surely by training,
maybe by nature, I killed
this slick of muscle
two yards long, raced
from the nave of white meat
its guts luminous

with junk, ate of the flesh
I flinched from. Now
I have another ambition.
Bulldogging it back
I hold on to the tail

while it swallows strength
of a darkness I know
only when gliding in surf
as in sleep, having
learned in danger
to commend myself

only to myself, predatory,
ascendant, at that threshold
we are now locked in,
forked, finned, sensing
again the tide's arterial
assault on the reef,
32

the glittering impress
of a menhaden school
panicking, the gasp
of polyp and tumultuous
sonar of plankton...
until we surge apart.

And I rise, caught
by the air, into all
surfaces shining by moonlight
where nothing is still
and the darkness is one dance,
one life, one love.

Ashore

I give the blue fog I've slept in
to the first being I meet:
a woman sleeping in the surf of dreams.
The night heron calls the west moon
from the corner of my eye.
I step back twice
& with my one good arm
let loose the hammerhead slewing in the otter trawl.
Firedrake of glacial pit, griefmistress
of the conger twilight,
I take back my love of land
lost when I first read these waters
covered variously with the pale luminescence of my fever.
I was hidden in the things I sought beneath it.
No matter: we have risen
& gone swimming & singing together.
Now I want to sit & think about it.
I want to hunker down & listen to her.
I want to hear her whole
in a sway of feathers, a swale of fog
when the wind is east & gusting
and I feel beyond my skin the other end
of dreaming,
falling moment to moment to the shape of the sea.

Off Moments

Hearing Helen Trauble, three days dead,
sing from a record played in her memory
the song "I'm only a bird in a gilded cage,"
I remember my mother, dead ten years,
telling and totalling her griefs thru the night
seated alone at the kitchen table while
in darkness I lay wondering why so much
must be said when so much must be done by day.
Then hearing her break into that song
I'd rise and help her get to bed at last.
Now I catch what is left of my breath
hearing this grand soprano belt out the tune
she liked to sing, they say, to herself
in off moments for thirty years.
O I know about noble women
in the darkness of my sight when songs
done to death must be sung again.

Shaving with a Dull Razor

Someday I shall lie down
& let it grow
luxuriantly, scratchily
as a xmass tree ready for burning.

Host to all that fashion denies,
gold teeth, chiggers, virgins,
a meadow long abandoned
to birds & rusting autobodies.

But now I scrape what resists & hides,
scars of old fights, capillaries
booze has exploded, shapeless fat
frying between a little skin & bone.

What is the will of bacteria?
What is the song of the gene? I ask,
carving my death mask, sighing for sleep.

Living on the Lower East Side During the Sixties:
Or the Triumph of Surrealism
over the Forces of Repression

Slovakin creep, Polack, Bohunk...
what's a good slur
for this sonovabitch downstairs
from...from east Europe!...who yells
beatnik hippiee bum & calls the cops
whenever I throw a party or a fit
& noise & plaster
rain on him & his churchgoing wife
& his three dopey, malnourished kids?

So the sink overflows.
I spritz him at the door: "Yo
no aspic englisha, chingara."
"I tall janitor goddamn ruggy crazy," he says.
"I kick your teeth out your ass," I say.
"--Listen, you can shovel gravel up it
only the faucet, fix it, neighbor."
"Ok, botchagaloop. Awwright! Lemme lone."
& he rolls his eyes. I roll my eyes.

So I yell with my family,
get high & stomp to loud music,
fall off bureaus, have friends
falling in at all hours
raising roofs & rents. So
his cops come to lean on my doorsill
while I swallow evidence & shit
bricks to light the world.

One night he got mugged in the vestibule
& I took him to Bellevue, his
nose like a rose flattened, mouth
spouting dialect & health cards,
his kids teeth his wifes mastectomy.
Going downtown later dawn overtook us
with pizzas & guitars geezing in the sky
as though the Fillmore still played on.

Another time his place was robbed
by a punk junkie I caught
with a broomhandle on the firecape,
who offered to turn me on
if I turned him loose, & kicked
me in the face when I mentioned motherhood,
while firemen dancing on the first floor
kicked out windows looking for fire,
Which came twice a year anyhow,
sweetening the management's longing
to get old people out of cheap apartments.
Then we'd stand in the street
barechested & bathrobed with
neighbors cheering the debris
cascading down on our popsciles.
Only the roaches were fireproof.

When we meet again, we're friends.
He didn't know I moved out years ago
to Westbeth, the Artist's Housing.
He didn't know I was an artist
but everybody in Westbeth does.
His wife & kids are fine, the hippies
gone & the Puerto Ricans second generation.
We congratulate each other on surviving

& look to see who's next in line
among the partygoers hopheading homeward,
the late hunters still trying to score,
the ex-nazi translating Nietzsche, highstepping
cats carrying tv's, the potbellied slumlords
in front of Ratner's who scratch, scratch
to the rhythem of a hot number
da diddie, die diddee, rup rup va va voom!

The Switch

In young sunlight
on my pale hand
a bug breaks open
two wisps of wings:
a watery gold
knits and beads
in the frets.

When it takes off
a speck of sun
remains, an undersea
glaze that turns
to a shiver,
felt last as a prism
sliding from my skin.

A Piece of the Action

Riding the IRT uptown
I saw a masher coming down

or what
do I call this guy, the hulk
of him two seats wide,

who in the nearly empty car
     plumps down next to a schoolgirl
     & sprawls against her
     & grins into his newspaper   .   The act so open,

               the girl's body
          suddenly tense, her face coming up
        startled, divining

                                   She shifts   .

                                   He shifts   .

       I frown
               & he grins back at me
                              not challenging
                              but welcoming me to
                              his pleasure

A freak?
A sadist? A
dirty prick?

Goddamnit, why dosn't she get up!

                              but just keeps staring away
                              acknowledging neither of us

Shall I say

      Miss, is this man bothering you?
  or
      Hey man! cut that shit out!
                              & if he still grins
                          go for him, fast
      so he can't
get to his feet   (I realize that would be a pleasure

      though old fashioned
                              but what's his?

Does he jack off later
remembering the warmth & curve against him
& climax
yelling
          HOT DOG!
                      or murmuring   is   o   bel
      or whispering
mama
    or moo-moo
                  or where's his other hand, maybe he's...

No, he's reading
his newspaper, still
grinning

42

&   the girl drops her eyes to her book
            her hair falls forward around her face
&   slouching a little
                    smiles to herself   smiles

(by this time, tho
it's none of my business, I'm
feeling left out,

            like the time the two girls I brought home
            started making it with each other

            & the time
            when at a conventional party
            Joe grinned deliriously
            & said, I'm an armpit man myself.

So I cross my legs
& start smiling, the three of us smiling,
to see what else is up, uptown, downtown,
all around the town,
some time after
the sexual revolution.

Muggings

The tough thing about screaming
is you can't tell
if it's a kid throwing a tantrum
or a teenager freaking out
or if someone in mortal terror
is uncorking a squeal, the pitch
unsexed and perfect.

You have to listen, anyhow,
a long time
walking block after block
to get why neon gravels gooseflesh
when sirens begin ricocheting and a crowd
hammerlocks a firetrap. Maybe for years
fingering money
you have to breathe streetlevel fumes
to suspect a smell disappearing
up a stairwell. Or backtrack a district
cops have deserted and detour
past meatracks of gay folk
where darkness spools on turbines
streaked with grit that rises, swirling, after subway trains.
And listen hard to steam escaping manholes
with an irregular chuff, sewers
echoing the river
that has swallowed a thunderstorm,
the graffiti phizzing off
in the faces of young girls as elevator doors
close behind them, the oaths

a cabbie mouths
to himself alone in the mirror, and footsteps
doubletiming your own. The moment it starts,
listen, ---cry poor!   ---cry mercy!
but take heart:
when the devil in the sky is whaling his wife
with one hand
and beating his bishop with the other,
then when you're out strolling
by the beautiful people you were born with,
and their dogs
underslung and overshot
sashay to your side
to nuzzle your wallet and your crotch,
then you can tell
New York has three sexes
whose wholeness is this darkness
you sleep in.

Inland Percussive

The piledriver
a block away makes
my pulse keep time. Firelines
in the nerves
flare & crackle, I steel myself
& still
I'm driven down, all of me
down.
          Often
on a mountain
stretched out empty
I've been compacted with flow
until I could swing with ridgelines,
overlap rock
& drift with one sustained beat
thru range to floodplain.

And I've caught the sea in my chest,
under my heart a star
seen at dawn
shines as I start
ebbing for twilight, countersinking
when the undersides
of things resting on the earth
also begin glowing.

But this is darkness firing
darkness. Darker & deeper
at night I rock in the after-shock
I feel darkness tunneling
thru sleeper above & below me
& the blister of my heart
collapses a column a blood thru twelve floors
down to the shields of earth colliding
underground.

46

Here

I get drunk
& want to throw
myself into the great fleeing
darkness I have heard
racing all day over the roof.
But a little girl
comes in with a nosebleed & says
Daddy! I'm dying

Sailing to Ireland

1

My aunt Gert, Brooklyn-born,
went daft at forty, raved
    of the Green Hornet
always following her, waiting his chance
to snatch her to his mountain castle
& keep her a slave to her dirty wishes
    forever & forever.

Dumped in Creedmore
she knew it was Ireland.
    Amazed
that we'd come so far to visit,
    she cried
        for us
who had to go back.

11

For me the West is finished.
For them---my relatives, irishamerican floozies, drifters,
wife-dodgers, gravediggers, diabetics
--it never was.
Sober they went to work or church
with sticks up their asses,
drunk they cursed god & work
& fought each other.
But like my mother who died of drink
in a hospital
not wanting to die
but wanting to come home,
none believed it.
48

111

In Brooklyn backyards some beer parties
still end in Ireland. Sopranos & tenors
start belting out the old tunes,
arguments subside into wistful stares,
& the company concedes the night.

& as voice by voice enters the summer air,
& old couples dry each other's tears,
& aunts croon to nephews steaming in their fat,
& uncles floored by boilermakers bubble thru their mustaches,

then what never was becomes the lost,
& home and homeland are reconciled.

1V

& if tonight I am drinking to your health,
my greeneyed darlings, to you & whoever
never crossed a sea or sought a land
but those charted by booze & madness,
I am also drinking to my death,
as my mother & father did to theirs,
singing & sailing open to the night
drowning this vast continent you
all rest in finally, unloved, unfound.

THE TIDEFALL WILDERNESS

Wind backing into the southwest
burrs new buds of the basswood;
deer faint forward
to the edge of the swamp.

Fogdogs
brightening. Spring
vanishing. In the hour before sunrise
April thru June
I wander in a birdsong   .

            The wind stops at the nearest tree
                    as if waiting to speak.
            A treetoad shifts its grip,
                        wide awake.

The stump of a leg is bared to the skier.
Autobodies roll in surf.
In gunkholes
ooze pushes forth a creamy froth
the hacklehead's call will sound from on on warm nights.

I step into the canoe of moonrise
& my shadow furs
with filings racing from the northern lights.
I step into a willow & shiver .

            Wind awakening
                    a girl's body before dawn,
            in purple space-warp returning
            a gull or girl
                        whispering
            at the end of song.   The lightfall . Dawn-song

Whitethroated sparrow
upswelling at field-edge   in the steep of the wave

          sleep   sleep   seas

If I could dance, bodysurf
my bow-wave with the moon tumbling,
haul, like Willis in his eleven-foot dingy,
the frail sail of myself across the Atlantic
steering the lotus in the foreknowledge
I'd one morning fall from the stern of the world,
even as I train, year on year, for the sea,
that I might know the quickening
of dolphin
rounding a point
a bight & a tide away,
& danced then, finally, a wave
in fulness on the ground of invisible earth,
in the good ship Chunderhara dithering loose as an eel,
still first I'd wander the wilderness
of birdsong & birdcry,
I'd know a world further than my own,
world further in passion
for people being broken
but thru this, maybe,
into song

I sleep without dreaming
but hear myself coming & going
I wake the seal's forty seconds
        counting stars by coal-fall.
I sport the wart
        with the hair of the moon,
the moon
        in the eye of an osprey:

I bark at stray dogs with the pheasant's glather
when I'm humble & fit, or this halfassed baying
for salami & tuna gets going
as gametrails slither beyond crossed lines of timber & tide

as dunes to the sea
I move as a lover   .

                    Then the stench of asphyxiated
                    hogchokers stinks up the wetlands.

                    All the wash on the clothesline goes crazy
                    waving goodbye

Blackburnian   Yellow   Black-throated Blue

Where do they go,
the few marine creatures I know
when they're stricken?
the mola nicked by a prop
sideswiping the swell,
the young hawksbill turtle
lost a hemisphere from summer...
when I lean
into the northeast wind, arms out
to catch what they cannot hold, as if
to take on a sea,
others in thicket & fog
bend with me, and on the deck I lurch
like the duck I saw with one foot
that a squalline overtook
down a hardscrabble dune: gone!

Keels bulge   bilges rot   rust hemmorhages

And I lean until darkness is leaping
for those who found death by water,
who went aground in heavy surf,
who fouled their nets,
who fell over soundlessly
& floated for hours or days or weeks until they drowned.

A niche shifts:
   a shoal disappears in a season,
       overnight in a gale,
fisherfolk gone, two generations vanished, tide
   scouring echochambers,
killifish, cunner, stickleback the red tide slaughters.
      Or the inward burning of the perriwinkle shell,
the last fold of summer tucking a girl
          & me in bed,
dark tan at moontide

earth unbegun in the wildest sense
                 in the commune of the sea

Floodtide
at twilight, I am in love with it.
Shall I ever leap over it?
I lie by a woman I love
& lie to myself: desiring desire's end.
I fish with my arms in the sky,
darkness rushing under my shoulders,
groundsharks showing white bellies
as they feed heavily upward
in the first glassy hump of the rip.

Darkness comes around
& the lighthouse wizens in a linesquall,
marshfog muffles the jacklighter.
Darkness is here
by tankers squelched in the long stalk of oilspills,
radar stricken in its cradle, lights out.
I drift with the darkness
tilting down, flooding in sheets & vast planes,
the light in my head
focusing the eye of a hawk, fog evaporating
to a flamelike sound reading fair
the great seas like moons under the ocean.
Into the heart of sound
darkness arrives, & the last thing I hear
is the sky closing inside
& I open, all sides & senses
rounding down to a stillness
& the darkness ceases. I am at sea.

Fish feeding on fish.
White froth on a flat sea.
Cataract in an eye, a god's.
But no god to pray to.

North & northeast
the skies blaze & the sea surges twice, I fall away,
the land falls away and water overfalls water,
we fall away, and the roads of the carfields, hardly true,
fall to the right & left thermoclines, and what I read
freewheeling this electrical dance moving from time
is the creaturely drift of one end of Long Island,
Whitman's Paumonok, athwart the Atlantic, astride two dolphins!

"...land of the great trees..."

"...how the seal play at the end of the ice."

"Dream is their only divinity...."

"White shark follows the pilot whale, sea after sea."

"...the great book of the underwaters on a shoal of moonlight
opening!...."

In the half-light of the wave
seeing itself for the first & last time
I surprise the children of sandpipers
              tottering into flight
itself a wave, a dune

As the peregrine I watch winter by
takes off
for Labrador   and alewives

processioned landward
coast in a foil of brainwaves
and mackerel jump gulfs, springing north

I carry in my side
a green unease
gotten when I swept over a reef
into a glade where a girl showed me my need of peoples:

Called to, I am soon slipping underwater.
Hailed ashore, I am shining with spawn.

So I turn in spring and live with the land.
Then I know what winter has made of my heart,
what has fed there & nested there,
what now from the height & speed of migrating falcons
stoops to behold it.

They make me a brother and ask me to speak.

And I long
to be turned again
witness to what wakes beyond me,
peoples of the bays & boglands, round dance of shoalwater,
fog at night lifting the abyssal plain's undermusic
as waterbirds restlessly move
      ---calls spilling forward, brief rushes,
           loons stuttering, shitepokes skidding foam,
the innominate thumpfucker I hear from a heath fifing
              ---trill! --trill! ---trill!
coons snuffing swaybacked mole tunnels,
timberdoodles at nuptials over
the resinous dusk of pine barrens,
tidewater that peat has given a coppery burnishing
deep down but only glancingly seen
a gull alighting beside me on the beach at night
a sleeping girl sighing.

I, tiderunner, fallen from the wave I rode brimming,
taking from what I love only the form of falling

have come back to tell thee Whitman the
sea is an open road.

The sea itself is survival.

A new wind begins
underwater. Lobsters scut
backwards, englished.
Static invades the sleep
of the rich, who go thru the motions
of burying the allies of children, buying
land. In the squid
a seed pivots north, toward the web
of winds. Shrimp
logroll a sleet of cellophane
thru the alewife gallery. In the embrace
of the starfish
the clam relaxes. In the embrace of a star
I am born
lame, I burn up.

And I dance

                    (many currents feed the Gulft Stream:
                    one is a woman's flow
                    another's an eagle's

Four are rivers,   Whale
fairways in amethyst interface   Squid
                                                    Jellyfish
                                                    Shark

One a spinoff of the eddy of Atlantis
        step twice into it & you glory with dolphins

This one is the song of the Americas
                                    a tribe of wings

This the girl who drives fisherman mad

                by day a stone by night an isle
                by summer a cave of stars
                shouldered by westering groundswells

...these are the underwaters, the unlearnt music
the salt of our cells will sing
when we darken.

                Spend a night-tide
                learning a new voice.
                By dawn you have a new trade)